Illinois' Firearm Concealed Carry Law FAQ Handbook
Part of the eBook Esquire Series

By Cameron R. Monti, Esq.

DISCLAIMER

You should not act based upon any information in this Illinois' Firearm Concealed Carry Law FAQ Handbook without first seeking the advice of professional legal counsel. *The information presented in this Firearm Concealed Carry Law FAQ Handbook is intended to be for informational purposes only and should not be construed, or relied on, as formal legal advice or the formation of a lawyer or attorney-client relationship*. This Illinois' Firearm Concealed Carry Law FAQ Handbook does not discuss in any great detail the legal requirements or prohibitions set forth under Illinois' Firearm Owners Identification Card Act [430 ILCS 65/0.01, *et seq*]. Therefore, readers are advised to review the Firearm Owners Identification Card Act to ensure compliance therein, as may be applicable and/or required under Illinois law. The author neither forms nor expresses any personal or political opinion or viewpoint as to the effectiveness or morality of the Illinois' Firearm Concealed Carry Act.

ABOUT THE AUTHOR

Cameron R. Monti is a Partner at the full-service Illinois law firm, Lavelle Law, Ltd. Cameron's law practice primarily focuses on the areas of corporate law, tax law, transactional law, and employment law matters. Cameron serves as an adjunct professor of law at John Marshall Law School (Chicago) teaching classes in the area of federal tax practice and procedure. In 2001, Cameron earned his law degree from Michigan State University College of Law, and in 2002, Cameron earned his LL.M. (Master of Laws) in Taxation Law from the University of Washington School of Law in Seattle, WA.

Cameron authored his first book in 2013 entitled *Illinois Medical Marijuana Law FAQ Handbook* as part of his eBook Esquire Series of legal FAQ handbooks and has made several live television appearances on WGN-TV9 News to discuss and explain new developments in Illinois law. Cameron currently resides in the Northwest suburbs of Illinois with his wife, Roxanne, and his two boys, Caden and Cole.

TABLE OF CONTENTS / INDEX

INTRODUCTION
Purpose of the Illinois' Firearm Concealed Carry Act   1-101
The reason why the Act approved and adopted   1-102
When did Act go into effect?   1-103
Oversight and enforcement of the Act   1-104
Permitted types of firearms   1-105
Prohibited firearms/weapons   1-106
Rights granted by Carry Conceal License ("License")   1-107

LICENSE ELIGIBILITY REQUIREMENTS
Eligibility requirement and qualifications for License   2-101
Eligibility of non-residents of Illinois   2-102
Classification of Illinois resident and non-resident   2-103

LICENSE APPLICATION REQUIREMENTS
Information required of Illinois resident applicants   3-101
Information required of out-of-state applicants   3-102
Rights of out-of-state residents (not residing in Illinois) under the Act   3-103
Background check   3-104
Confidentiality of application information   3-105
Providing dishonest or misleading application information   3-106
How long is a License valid?   3-107
Waiting period for application determination   3-108
Basis for denying an application   3-109
Refund of fees   3-110
Renewing License   3-111

FIREARMS TRAINING
Required firearms training as part of application process   4-101
Firearms Training for renewal License   4-102
Basis for denying issuance of certificate of completion   4-103
Firearms record retention and disclosure   4-104
Exemption from firearms training   4-105
Credit for prior firearms training   4-106

APPEALING LICENSE DECISIONS & THE REVIEW BOARD
Appealing a denied License   5-101
Appealing a revoked or suspended License   5-102
The Concealed Carry Licensing Review Board   5-103
Basis for unsuccessfully appealing for issuance of a License by Review Board   5-104
Review Board meeting requirement to review objections to License applications   5-105
Confidentiality of License application appealed to Review Board   5-106
Process and Procedure of an objection and appeal to the Review Board   5-107
Time period for Review Board determination on an objection   5-108
Right to attend Review Board meetings   5-109
Appeal rights of Review Board determination   5-110

Basis for suing Illinois State Police, law enforcement agency or Review Board   5-111
Check and balances for oversight of Review Board   5-112

REVIEW BOARD COMPOSITION & TERMS
Term limits for Review Board   6-101
Composition of the Review Board   6-102

COMPLIANCE OBLIGATIONS AFTER GRANT OF LICENSE
Licensee's carry obligation   7-101
Notice of moving or change of residence   7-102
Change of legal name   7-103
Notice requirement for lost, stolen, or destroyed License   7-104
Purchasing or selling firearms   7-105

TRAFFIC & INVESTIGATORY STOPS BY POLICE
Traffic stops and notification of concealed firearm   8-101
Passenger obligations   8-102

PROHIBITED AREAS OF FIREARMS
Prohibited areas for firearms   9-101
Firearms in vehicles/parking lot exception   9-102

SCHOOLS, COLLEGES & UNIVERSITIES
Right to prohibit, limit, or allow firearms and reporting requirements   10-101

PRIVATE PROPERTY OWNERS - RIGHTS & OBLIGATIONS
Right to prohibit or allow firearms   11-101

FEES & FISCAL ACCOUNTABILITY
Fees and where they are apportioned   12-101

VIOLATIONS, REVOCATIONS & SUSPENSIONS
Basis for violations, revocations, and suspensions of License   13-101
Right to appeal revocations, and suspensions of License   13-102
Uncertified firearms training instructors   13-103

CERTIFIED FIREARMS TRAINING INSTRUCTOR QUALIFICATIONS
Requirements to become a certified firearms training instructor   14-101
Denial or revocation of certification to be an approved firearms training instructor   14-102
Uncertified firearms training instructors   14-102

LOCAL GOVERNMENTS
Limits on local governments to exercise Home Rule to restrict concealed carry firearms   15-101

CONCEALED CARRY LICENSE AND THE FOID CARD
Plan of consolidation of FOID Card and License   16-101

INTRODUCTION

1-101. What is the purpose of Illinois' Firearm Concealed Carry Act?

Illinois' Firearm Concealed Carry Act ("**Act**") provides its citizens, who have a valid Concealed Carry License ("**License**"), the lawful right to carry certain concealed firearms on his/her person.

1-102. Why did the State of Illinois approve and adopt Illinois' Firearm Concealed Carry Act?

The State of Illinois was ordered by a U.S. Court of Appeals for the Seventh Circuit to adopt legislation regulating the right to carry concealed firearms within six months as a consequence of its ruling that held the concealed carry ban in the State of Illinois was unconstitutional under the Second Amendment of the United States Constitution.

1-103. When did the Illinois' Firearm Concealed Carry Act go into effect?

The Act went into effect on July 9, 2013. The State of Illinois was the last state to adopt concealed firearm laws.

1-104. Who oversees the enforcement of the Act, and who is delegated the authority to grant or deny a License to carry a concealed firearm?

The Illinois State Police and the Concealed Carry Licensing Review Board are granted the power to either grant or deny a License. The Illinois State Police, in consultation with and subject to the approval of the Chief Procurement Officer, may procure a single contract or multiple contracts to implement the provisions of the Act. The Illinois State Police are required to adopt rules to implement the provisions of the Act. The Illinois State Police may adopt rules necessary to implement the provisions of the Act through the use of emergency rulemaking (in accordance with Section 5-45 of the Illinois Administrative Procedure Act [See, 5 ILCS 100/5-45] for a period no later than January 5, 2014) [430 ILCS 66/95(a) and (b)].

1-105. What kind of concealed firearm is lawfully permitted under the Act?

The Act states that a "concealed firearm" means a loaded or unloaded handgun carried on or about a person completely or mostly concealed from view of the public or on or about a person within a vehicle. Subject to certain exclusions set forth under the Act, a "handgun" means any device which is designed to expel a projectile or projectiles by the action of an explosion, expansion of gas, or escape of gas that is designed to be held and fired by the use of a single hand [430 ILCS 66/5].

1-106. What kinds of firearms/weapons are not allowed under the Act?

The Act lists specific weapons that are *not* considered a "handgun," and therefore, cannot be lawfully carried and concealed under the Act: (1) stun gun or taser; (2) a machine gun; (3) a short-barreled rifle; (4) shotgun; (5) any pneumatic gun; (6) spring gun; (7) paint ball gun; and (8) B-B gun which expels a single globular projectile not exceeding .18 inch in diameter, or which has a maximum muzzle velocity of less than 700 feet per second, or which expels breakable paint balls containing washable marking colors [430 ILCS 66/5(1) - (4)].

If there is a question as to whether a particular type weapon can be lawfully carried and/or concealed under the Act, and it is not listed as one of the specific exclusions under the Act, the reader is advised to contact an attorney or the Illinois State Police for further guidance.

1-107. What does a License allow a person to do under the Act?

A License lawfully authorizes a person to carry a loaded or unloaded concealed firearm, fully concealed or partially concealed, on or about his or her person; and (2) keep or carry a loaded or unloaded concealed firearm on or about his or her person within a vehicle [430 ILCS 66/10(c)(1) and (2)]. This assumes that a License is granted after a Licensee has properly satisfied all requirements and qualifications under the Act – one major prerequisite of which is having a valid Firearm Owner's Identification (**"FOID"**) Card pursuant to Illinois' Firearm Owners Identification Card Act (**"FOID Card Act"**) [430 ILCS 65/0.01, *et seq*]. It is important for the reader to understand that the FOID Card is *not* a Conceal and Carry License (card). ***Therefore, for any Illinois resident interested in lawfully carrying a concealed firearm in the State of Illinois (in accordance with the restrictions and obligations under the Act), an Illinois resident must receive two (2) different items under Illinois law: (1) the FOID Card; and (2) the Concealed Carry License.***

It is worth noting that the Illinois State Police website notes in its Frequently Asked Question section that current peace officers and retired police officers eligible under a federally approved retired officer concealed carry program such as the Illinois Retired Officer Concealed Carry (IROCC) Program do not need to apply for a License to lawfully carry a concealed firearm.

LICENSE ELIGIBILITY REQUIREMENTS

2-101. What are the requirements and qualifications to be eligible for a License?

The Illinois State Police must issue a License to an applicant if such applicant:

(1) is at least 21-years-old;

(2) has a currently valid FOID Card and at the time of application meets the requirements for the issuance of a FOID Card and is not prohibited under the FOID Card Act or federal law from possessing or receiving a firearm (NOTE: *No person may legally acquire or possess any firearm or firearm ammunition unless he or she first qualifies for and is issued a valid FOID Card*);

(3) has not been convicted or found guilty in Illinois or in any other state of: (A) a misdemeanor involving the use or threat of physical force or violence to any person within the five (5) years preceding the date of the License application; or (B) two (2) or more violations related to driving while under the influence of alcohol, other drug or drugs, intoxicating compound or compounds, or any combination thereof, within the five (5) years preceding the date of the License application;

(4) is not the subject of a pending arrest warrant, prosecution, or proceeding for an offense or action that could lead to disqualification to own or possess a firearm;

(5) has not been in residential or court-ordered treatment for alcoholism, alcohol detoxification, or drug treatment within the five (5) years immediately preceding the date of the License application;

(6) has completed Firearms Training and any education component required under Section 75 of the Act (which includes, among other things, at least sixteen (16) hours of specific Firearms Training);

(7) has provided the application and documentation required in Section 30 of the Act;

(8) has submitted the requisite $150 application fee (as of 2014) ; and

(9) does not pose a danger to himself, herself, or others, or a threat to public safety as determined by the Concealed Carry Licensing Review Board in accordance with Section 20 [430 ILCS 66/10 and 430 ILCS 66/60(b)].

2-102. Is a non-resident of Illinois eligible to apply for a License?

Yes, non-resident from any state or territory of the United States License is permitted to submit a License application so long as the Illinois State Police determine that the laws related to firearm ownership, possession, and carrying of the non-resident's home state are substantially similar to the requirements to obtain a License under Illinois' Act [430 ILCS 66/40(b) and (c)].

2-103. Who considered an Illinois resident versus a non-resident for purposes of applying for a License?

The Act defines a "non-resident" as a person who has not resided within Illinois for more than thirty (30) days and resides in another state or territory [430 ILCS 66/40(a)].

LICENSE APPLICATION REQUIREMENTS

3-101. What information does the License application request or require of an applicant who is a resident of Illinois?

Applicants seeking a License can apply online by visiting Concealed Carry License webpage of the Illinois State Police website: https://ccl4illinois.com/ccw/public/home.aspx (visited 01/20/2014). The License application contains, requires, or requests the following information:

(1) the applicant's name, current address, date and year of birth, place of birth, height, weight, hair color, eye color, maiden name or any other name the applicant has used or identified with, and any address where the applicant resided for more than thirty (30) days within the ten (10) years preceding the date of the License application;

(2) the applicant's valid driver's license number or valid state identification card number;

(3) a waiver of the applicant's privacy and confidentiality rights and privileges under all federal and state laws, including those limiting access to juvenile court, criminal justice, psychological, or psychiatric records or records relating to any institutionalization of the applicant, and an affirmative request that a person having custody of any of these records provide it or information concerning it to the Illinois State Police;

(4) an affirmation that the applicant possesses a currently valid FOID Card and card number if possessed or notice the applicant is applying for a Firearm Owner's Identification Card in conjunction with the License application;

(5) an affirmation that the applicant has not been convicted or found guilty of: (A) a felony; (B) a misdemeanor involving the use or threat of physical force or violence to any person within the five (5) years preceding the date of the application; or (C) two (2) or more violations related to driving while under the influence of alcohol, other drug or drugs, intoxicating compound or compounds, or any combination thereof, within the five (5) years preceding the date of the License application;

(6) whether the applicant has failed a drug test for a drug for which the applicant did not have a prescription, within the previous year, and if so, the provider of the test, the specific substance involved, and the date of the test;

(7) written consent for the Illinois State Police to review and use the applicant's Illinois digital driver's license or Illinois identification card photograph and signature;

(8) a full set of fingerprints submitted to the Illinois State Police in electronic format, provided the Illinois State Police may accept an application submitted without a set of fingerprints in which case the Illinois State Police must be granted thirty (30) days in addition to the ninety (90) days provided under subsection (e) of Section 10 of the Act to issue or deny a License;

(9) a head and shoulder color photograph in a size specified by the Illinois State Police taken within the thirty (30) days preceding the date of the License application; and

(10) a photocopy of any certificates or other evidence of compliance with the training requirements under the Act [430 ILCS 66/30(b)(1) – (10)].

3-102. What information does the License application request or require of an out-of-state resident (i.e., not a resident of Illinois) applicant?

A non-resident applicant must apply to the Illinois State Police and must satisfy all of the same qualifications (as set forth and further described in Section 25 of the Act) as an Illinois resident seeking a License, with, of course, the exception of the Illinois residency requirement (of the FOID Card Act).

A non-resident applicant must submit the following: (1) the application and documentation required under Section 30 of the Act and the $300 non-resident application fee (as of 2014); (2) a notarized document stating that the applicant: (A) is eligible under federal law and the laws of his or her home state or territory of residence to own or possess a firearm; (B) if applicable, has a license or permit to carry a firearm or concealed firearm issued by his or her home state or territory of residence and attach a copy of the license or permit to the application; (C) understands Illinois laws pertaining to the possession and transport of firearms; and (D) acknowledges that the applicant is subject to the jurisdiction of the Illinois State Police and Illinois courts for any violation of the Act; (3) a photocopy of any certificates or other evidence of compliance with the training requirements under Section 75 of the Act; (4) a head and shoulder color photograph in a size specified by the Illinois State Police taken within the thirty (30) days preceding the date of the application; (5) a driver's license or identification card from his or her home state or territory of residence; and (6) In lieu of a valid Firearm Owner's Identification Card, the applicant must submit documentation and information required by the Illinois State Police to obtain a Firearm Owner's Identification Card, including an affidavit that the non-resident meets the mental health standards to obtain a firearm under Illinois law, and the Illinois State Police must ensure that the applicant would meet the eligibility criteria to obtain a Firearm Owner's Identification card if he or she was a resident of Illinois [430 ILCS 66/40(c) and (d) and 430 ILCS 66/60(c)].

3-103. For non-residents of Illinois (who hold a valid license to carry a concealed firearm from his or her home state), what rights do non-residents have to carry a concealed firearm within permitted areas inside the State of Illinois?

Nothing in the Act prohibits a non-resident from transporting a concealed firearm within his or her vehicle in the State of Illinois, so long as the concealed firearm remains within his or her vehicle *and* the non-resident: (1) is not prohibited from owning or possessing a firearm under federal law; (2) is eligible to carry a firearm in public under the laws of his or her home state or territory (as evidenced by the possession of a concealed carry license or permit issued by his or her state of residence, if applicable); and (3) is not in possession of a License under the Act; and (4) if the non-resident leaves his or her vehicle unattended, he or she must store the firearm within a locked vehicle or locked container within the vehicle in accordance with subsection (b) of Section 65 of the Act [430 ILCS 66/40(e)].

3-104. How extensive is the background check related to the License application process?

The Illinois State Police must conduct a background check of all applicants to ensure compliance with the requirements of the Act and all federal, Illinois, and local laws. The background check will include a search of the following: (1) the National Instant Criminal Background Check System of the Federal Bureau of Investigation (FBI); (2) all available state and local criminal history record information files, including records of juvenile adjudications; (3) all available federal, state, and local records regarding wanted persons; (4) all available federal, state, and local records of domestic violence restraining and protective orders; (5) the files of the Illinois Department of Human Services relating to mental health and developmental disabilities; (6) all other available records of a federal, state, or local agency or other public entity in any jurisdiction likely to contain information relevant to whether the applicant is prohibited from purchasing, possessing, or carrying a firearm under federal, state, or local law; and (7) Fingerprints will be checked against the current and future Illinois State Police and FBI criminal history record databases. The Illinois State Police will charge License applicants a fee for conducting the criminal history records check (of which fee cannot exceed the actual cost of the records check), which must be deposited in the State Police Services Fund [430 ILCS 66/35(1) – (7)].

3-105. Will the information I provide in my License application be kept confidential? Who can access it?

Within ten (10) days of its receipt of a completed application, the Illinois State Police must enter the application information within its database [430 ILCS 66/10(j)]. The Illinois State Police must maintain the database of all License applicants and Licensees. The database is available to all federal, State, and local law enforcement agencies, State's Attorneys, the Illinois Attorney General, and authorized court personnel. The database is searchable and will provide all information included in a person's application, including the applicant's previous addresses within the ten (10) years prior to the License application and any information related to violations of the Act. No law enforcement agency, State's Attorney, Illinois Attorney General, or member or staff of the judiciary may lawfully provide any information to a requester unless they are entitled to receive it by law [430 ILCS 66/10(i)].

3-106. What happens if an applicant is not completely truthful or is misleading with the information provided in a License application?

When an applicant files a License application, the applicant submits the License application "under penalty of perjury." More specifically, applicants will see on the License application form the following statement printed in bold type: "Warning: Entering false information on this form is punishable as perjury under Section 32-2 of the Criminal Code of 2012." Therefore, applicants are required to be truthful and cannot provide misleading or fraudulent information [430 ILCS 66/30(a)].

3-107. How long is a License valid?

A License is valid throughout the State of Illinois for a period of five (5) years from the date of issuance [430 ILCS 66/10(c)].

3-108. How long does an applicant have to wait to receive a decision from the Illinois State Police on his or her License application?

The Act requires that the Illinois State Police either issue or deny an applicant a License within ninety (90) days of receipt of a fully completed application (and receipt of payment of the requisite application fee) [430 ILCS 66/10(e)], unless the 90-day period is tolled as a result of the referral of an objection to the issuance of a License (by a law enforcement agency) to the Concealed Carry Licensing Review Board. In such case, the 90-day period is tolled during the period of review and until the Concealed Carry Licensing Review Board issues its decision [430 ILCS 66/15(c)]. If the Illinois State Police fails to make any timely determination within ninety (90) days (and the Board is not involved), an applicant has the right to appeal to the Director of the Illinois State Police for a hearing [430 ILCS 66/87(a)].

3-109. What are some of the ways a License application can be denied by the Illinois State Police?

The Illinois State Police must deny an applicant a License if the Applicant fails to meet any of the application requirements or qualifications under the Act, or the Illinois State Police receives a determination from the Concealed Carry Licensing Review Board that the applicant is ineligible for a License [430 ILCS 66/10(f)]. The Illinois State Police website (visited on 01/20/2014) noted that during their first round of application submissions, over 100 applications were deemed incomplete and rejected due to missing information, insufficient training, invalid or missing photo, and/or failure to provide ten (10) years of residence information.

3-110. Can an applicant for a License obtain a refund of the application fee, replacement fee, or renewal application fee if the applicant changes his or her mind, or if the application is denied by the Illinois State Police or Review Board?

No, application, renewal, and replacement fees paid are non-refundable [430 ILCS 66/60(a)].

3-111. How often does a Licensee need to *renew* his or her License?

Yes, License is valid for a five (5) year period. Therefore, a License must be renewed every five (5) years to have a valid License for an additional period of five (5) years. The renewal application must contain the information required in Section 30 of the Act, with the exception of fingerprints – an renewal applicant need not resubmit a set of fingerprints. A Licensee seeking a renewal License must: (1) complete a renewal application; (2) complete three (3) hours of training required under Section 75 of this Section; (3) pay the applicable renewal fee ($150 for Illinois residents or $300 for non-residents, as of 2014); and (4) complete of an investigation under Section 35 of the Act. Applications to renewal a License must be made by completing and submitting the License renewal application to the Illinois State Police [430 ILCS 66/50 and 430 ILCS 66/10(c)].

FIREARMS TRAINING

4-101. Other than completion and submission of a *new* License application and payment of the applicable application fee, is any firearm training required?

Yes, a new License applicant must provide proof of completion of a firearms training course or combination of courses approved by the Illinois State Police ("**Firearms Training**") with a Concealed Carry Firearm Training Certificate signed by the certified training instructor and applicant. The Illinois State Police maintains a registry/database that includes information regarding Illinois State Police-approved firearm training instructors and a list of approved courses on the Illinois State Police website (visit: http://www.isp.state.il.us/ for more information).

A new License applicant must complete at least sixteen (16) hours of Firearms Training, which includes Range Qualification Time (as explained below) that covers the following:

(1) firearm safety;

(2) the basic principles of marksmanship;

(3) care, cleaning, loading, and unloading of a concealable firearm;

(4) all applicable State and federal laws relating to the ownership, storage, carry, and transportation of a firearm; and

(5) instruction on the appropriate and lawful interaction with law enforcement while transporting or carrying a concealed firearm [430 ILCS 66/75(b)].

Range Qualification Time: An applicant for a new License must provide proof of certification by a certified instructor that the applicant passed a live fire exercise with a concealable firearm consisting of: (1) a minimum of 30 rounds; and (2) 10 rounds from a distance of 5 yards; 10 rounds from a distance of 7 yards; and 10 rounds from a distance of 10 yards at a B-27 silhouette target approved by the Illinois State Police [430 ILCS 66/75(c)].

4-102. Is any Firearms Training required for a *renewal* License application?

Yes, an applicant for *renewal* of a License must provide proof of completion of a Firearms Training (as defined above) of at least three (3) hours [430 ILCS 66/75(d)].

4-103. Upon what basis, if any, can a Firearms Training instructor refuse or deny the issuance of a certificate of completion to a new or renewal License applicant?

A Firearms Training instructor must deny or refuse the issuance of a certificate of completion for a Firearm Training course if a student/applicant: (1) does not follow the orders of the certified firearms instructor; (2) in the judgment of the certified instructor, handles a firearm in a manner that poses a danger to the student/applicant or to others; or (3) during the range firing portion of testing the student/applicant fails to hit the target with at least seventy percent (70%) of the ammunition rounds fired [430 ILCS 66/75(e)].

4-104. How long are students'/applicants' Firearms Training records of kept and can the records be disclosed to anyone?

A Firearms Training instructor must maintain a record of each applicant/student's performance for at least five (5) years, and must make all records available upon demand of authorized personnel of Illinois State Police [430 ILCS 66/75(f)].

4-105. Do active members of law enforcement have to complete Firearms Training?

The following individuals are *exempt* from the Firearms Training requirement under the Act if the following are true:

(1) A person who has qualified to carry a firearm as an active law enforcement or corrections officer has successfully completed firearms training as required by his or her law enforcement agency and is authorized by his or her agency to carry a firearm; or

(2) A person currently certified as a firearms instructor by the Act or by the Illinois Law Enforcement Training Standards Board; or

(3) A person who has completed the required Firearms Training and has been issued a firearm control card by the Illinois Department of Financial and Professional Regulation [430 ILCS 66/75(h)].

4-106. Is anyone eligible for previously completed firearm training hours to be applied towards the sixteen (16) hours of Firearm Training required under the Act?

Yes, the Illinois State Police and certified firearms instructors must recognize eight (8) hours of training as completed toward the sixteen (16) hours of Firearm Training requirement if the applicant is an active, retired, or honorably discharged member of the U.S. Armed Forces. Any remaining hours that the applicant completes must at least cover the classroom subject matter regarding all applicable State and federal laws relating to the ownership, storage, carry, and transportation of a firearm, and the Range Qualification (See below)[430 ILCS 66/75(i)].

The Illinois State Police and certified firearms instructors must recognize up to eight (8) hours of training already completed toward the sixteen (16) hour Firearm Training requirement if the training course is approved by the Illinois State Police and was completed in connection with the applicant's previous employment as a law enforcement or corrections officer. Any remaining hours that the applicant completes must at least cover the classroom subject matter regarding all applicable State and federal laws relating to the ownership, storage, carry, and transportation of a firearm, and the Range Qualification (See below). A former law enforcement or corrections officer seeking Firearm Training credit for hours under this subsection must provide evidence that he or she separated from employment in good standing from each law enforcement agency where he or she was employed. An applicant who was discharged from a law enforcement agency for misconduct or disciplinary reasons is not eligible for credit under this subsection [430 ILCS 66/75(j)].

RANGE QUALIFICATION: An applicant for a new License must provide proof of certification by a certified instructor that the applicant passed a live fire exercise with a concealable firearm consisting of: (1) a minimum of 30 rounds; and (2) 10 rounds from a distance of 5 yards; 10 rounds from a distance of 7 yards; and 10 rounds from a distance of 10 yards at a B-27 silhouette target approved by the Illinois State Police [430 ILCS 66/75(c)].

APPEALING LICENSE DECISIONS & THE REVIEW BOARD

5-101. Does an applicant have any appeal rights if his or her application for a License is denied?

The Illinois State Police must notify an applicant stating the grounds for the denial of the License application. The notice of denial must advise the applicant of his or her right to an appeal through administrative and judicial review [430 ILCS 66/10(f)]. For administrative reviews, an applicant has the right to appeal to the Director of the Illinois State Police for a hearing if the applicant's License application is denied [430 ILCS 66/87(a)]. All final administrative decisions of the Illinois State Police or the Concealed Carry Licensing Review Board under the Act is subject to judicial review under the provisions of the Administrative Review Law [430 ILCS 66/87(b)].

5-102. Does an applicant have any appeal rights in the event of a revoked or suspended License?

Yes, whenever a License is revoked or suspended, the aggrieved party may appeal to the Director of the Illinois State Police for a hearing [430 ILCS 66/87(a)].

5-103. What is the Concealed Carry Licensing Review Board?

Concealed Carry Licensing Review Board is the Board within the Illinois State Police Department which was created under the Act to consider any objection to an applicant's eligibility to obtain a License. An objection, including any information relevant to the objection, may be submitted by a law enforcement agency or the Illinois State Police (pursuant to Section 15 of the Act) based upon a reasonable suspicion that the applicant is a danger to himself or herself or others, or a threat to public safety [430 ILCS 66/15(a)]. The Concealed Carry Licensing Review Board consists of seven (7) commissioners appointed by the Governor of Illinois (with the advice and consent of the Senate). Three (3) commissioners must reside within the First Judicial District and one (1) commissioner must reside within each of the four (4) remaining Judicial Districts.

No more than four (4) commissioners can be members of the same political party. The Governor of Illinois must designate one commissioner as the Chairperson [430 ILCS 66/20(a)].

5-104. What basis would the Concealed Carry Licensing Review Board determine an applicant is ineligible for a License?

Any law enforcement agency may submit an objection to a License applicant based upon a reasonable suspicion that the applicant is a danger to himself or herself or others, or a threat to public safety. If a law enforcement agency submits an objection within thirty (30) days after the entry of an applicant into the database, the Illinois State Police must submit the objection and all information available to the Concealed Carry Licensing Review Board under State and federal law related to the application to the Board within ten (10) days of completing all necessary background checks [430 ILCS 66/15(a)].

If an applicant has five (5) or more arrests, for any reason, that have been entered into the Criminal History Records Information (CHRI) System, within the seven (7) years prior to the date of application for a License, or has three (3) or more arrests within the seven (7) years preceding the date of application for a License for any combination of gang-related offenses, the Illinois State Police must object and submit the applicant's arrest record to the extent the Concealed Carry Licensing Review Board is allowed to receive that information under State and federal law, the application materials, and any additional information submitted by a law enforcement agency to the Board. For purposes of this subsection, "gang-related offense" is an offense described in Section 12-6.4, Section 24-1.8, Section 25-5, Section 33-4, or Section 33G-4, or in paragraph (1) of subsection (a) of Section 12-6.2, paragraph (2) of subsection (b) of Section 16-30, paragraph (2) of subsection (b) of Section 31-4, or item (iii) of paragraph (1.5) of subsection (i) of Section 48-1 of the Criminal Code of 2012 [430 ILCS 66/15(b)].

5-105. How often is the Concealed Carry Licensing Review Board required to meet to review objections to applications?

The Concealed Carry Licensing Review Board must meet at the call of the Board chairperson as often as necessary to consider objections to applications for a License under the Act. If necessary to ensure the participation of a commissioner, the Board must allow a commissioner to participate in a Concealed Carry Licensing Review Board meeting by electronic communication. Any commissioner participating electronically will be deemed present for purposes of establishing a quorum and voting [430 ILCS 66/20(c)].

5-106. Is the information provided by an applicant in a License application confidential even if it is sent to the Concealed Carry Licensing Review Board for review?

Yes, with one exception. All Concealed Carry Licensing Review Board decisions and voting records must be kept confidential and all materials considered by the Board are exempt from inspection, except upon order of a court [430 ILCS 66/20(d)].

5-107. What is the process and procedure when the Concealed Carry Licensing Review Board reviews an objection by a law enforcement agency in an effort to deny a License Application?

In considering an objection of a law enforcement agency or the Illinois State Police, the Concealed Carry Licensing Review Board is required to review the materials received with the objection. By a vote of at least four (4) Board commissioners, the Concealed Carry Licensing Review Board may request additional information from the law enforcement agency, Illinois State Police, or the applicant, or the testimony of the any of the foregoing parties. The Board may require that the applicant submit electronic fingerprints to Illinois State Police for an updated background check where the Board determines it lacks sufficient information to determine eligibility. The Concealed Carry Licensing Review Board may only consider information submitted by the Illinois State Police, a law enforcement agency, or the applicant. The Board must review each objection and determine by a majority vote of commissioners whether an applicant is eligible for a License [430 ILCS 66/20(e)].

5-108. How long does the Concealed Carry Licensing Review Board have to make a determination on whether or not to grant a License application in spite of the existence of an objection of a law enforcement agency or the Illinois State Police?

Generally, the Concealed Carry Licensing Review Board must issue a decision within thirty (30) days of receipt of the objection from the Illinois State Police. However, the Board is not required to issue a decision within the thirty (30) day time period if: (1) the Board requests information from the applicant, including but not limited to electronic fingerprints to be submitted to the Illinois State Police, in which case the Board is then given a time extension to render a decision within thirty (30) days of receipt of the required information from the applicant; (2) the applicant agrees, in writing, to allow the Board additional time to consider an objection; or (3) the Board notifies the applicant and the Illinois State Police that the Board needs an additional thirty (30) days to issue a decision [430 ILCS 66/20(f)(1) – (3)].

5-109. How does the Concealed Carry Licensing Review Board determine whether or not to grant or deny an applicant's License application in light of an objection or objections being filed by law enforcement?

If the Concealed Carry Licensing Review Board determines *by a preponderance of the evidence* that the applicant poses a danger to himself or herself or others, or is a threat to public safety, then the Concealed Carry Licensing Review Board must affirm the objection of the law enforcement agency or the Illinois State Police. Therefore, the Concealed Carry Licensing Review Board is then required to notify the Illinois State Police that the applicant is ineligible for a License. However, if the Concealed Carry Licensing Review Board does not conclude by a preponderance of the evidence that the applicant poses a danger to himself or herself or others, or does not determine the applicant is a threat to public safety, then the Concealed Carry Licensing Review Board must notify the Illinois State Police that the applicant is, in fact, eligible for a License [430 ILCS 66/20(g)].

5-110. Does an applicant have a legal right to attend any of the meetings of the Concealed Carry Licensing Review Board, or at minimum, could I require the Board to furnish me with copies of the books and records of the Board (pursuant to the Freedom of Information Act)?

No, meetings of the Concealed Carry Licensing Review Board are not subject to the Open Meetings Act and records of the Concealed Carry Licensing Review Board are not subject to the Freedom of Information Act [430 ILCS 66/20(h)].

5-111. Does an applicant have the right to appeal a decision to deny a License by the Concealed Carry Licensing Review Board?

Yes, an applicant has the right to petition the Illinois Circuit Court in writing (in the county of his or her residence) for a hearing upon the denial of the applicant's License application by the Concealed Carry Licensing Review Board [430 ILCS 66/87(a)].

5-112. Can an applicant sue the Concealed Carry Licensing Review Board, Illinois State Police, or other law enforcements agencies (or their employees) if there is reason to believe that the applicant's License application was denied on an improper basis, or a License was improperly granted to an applicant?

The Concealed Carry Licensing Review Board, Illinois State Police, local law enforcement agency, and/or the employees and agents of the foregoing who participate in the Licensing review or determination process under the Act cannot be held liable for damages in any civil action (lawsuit) arising from alleged wrongful or improper granting, denying, renewing, revoking, suspending, or failing to grant, deny, renew, revoke, or suspend a License under the Act, *except* for instances of proven willful or wanton misconduct [430 ILCS 66/45].

5-113. Are there any "checks and balances" to make sure the Concealed Carry Licensing Review Board is properly fulfilling its obligations under the Act?

Yes, the Concealed Carry Licensing Review Board must report monthly to the Governor of Illinois and the General Assembly on the number of objections received by the Board, and provide details of the circumstances in which the Concealed Carry Licensing Review Board has determined to deny an applicant's License based on law enforcement or Illinois State Police objections (under Section 15 of the Act). The report will not contain any identifying information about the applicants [430 ILCS 66/20(i)].

REVIEW BOARD COMPOSITION & TERMS

6-101. Are there term limitations that a commissioner can serve on the Concealed Carry Licensing Review Board?

The initial terms of the commissioners end on January 12, 2015. Thereafter, the commissioners will hold office for four (4) years, with terms expiring on the second Monday in January of the fourth year. Commissioners may be reappointed. Vacancies in the office of commissioner must be filled in the same manner as the original appointment, for the remainder of the unexpired term. The Governor of Illinois may remove a commissioner for incompetence, neglect of duty, malfeasance, or inability to serve. Commissioners must receive compensation in an amount equal to the compensation of members of the Executive Ethics Commission and may be reimbursed for reasonable expenses actually incurred in the performance of their Board duties, from funds appropriated for that purpose [430 ILCS 66/20(b)].

6-102. Who makes up the Concealed Carry Licensing Review Board?

The Act requires that the Concealed Carry Licensing Review Board must consist of: (1) one (1) commissioner with at least five (5) years of service as a federal judge; (2) two (2) commissioners with at least five (5) years of experience serving as an attorney with the U.S. Department of Justice; (3) three (3) commissioners with at least five (5) years of experience as a federal agent or employee with investigative experience or duties related to criminal justice under the U.S. Department of Justice, Drug Enforcement Administration (DEA), Department of Homeland Security, or Federal Bureau of Investigation (FBI); and (4) one (1) member with at least five (5) years of experience as a licensed physician or clinical psychologist with expertise in the diagnosis and treatment of mental illness [430 ILCS 66/20(a)(1) – (4)].

COMPLIANCE OBLIGATIONS AFTER GRANT OF LICENSE

7-101. After the issuance of a License to carry a concealed firearm. Does a Licensee always have to carry his or her License?

The general answer is YES. However, there are three (3) instances where a Licensee does NOT need to carry his or her License: (1) when the Licensee is carrying or possessing a concealed firearm on his or her land or in his or her abode, legal dwelling, or fixed place of business, or on the land or in the legal dwelling of another person as an invitee with that person's permission; (2) when the person is authorized to carry a firearm under Section 24-2 of the Criminal Code of 2012, except subsection (a-5) of that Section; or (3) when the handgun is broken down in a non-functioning state, is not immediately accessible, or is unloaded and enclosed in a case [430 ILCS 66/10(g)(1) – (3)].

7-102. What obligations does an Licensee have if he or she is moving, if any?

A Licensee is required to notify the Illinois State Police within thirty (30) days of moving or changing residence. The Licensee must submit a notarized statement indicating that the Licensee has changed his or her residence, must including the prior and current address and the date the applicant moved, and pay the requisite $75 fee (as of 2014) [430 ILCS 66/55(a) and 430 ILCS 66/60(d)]. A violation of the change of address notice requirement by a Licensee is a petty offense with a fine of $150 [430 ILCS 66/55(c)].

7-103. A Licensee's legal name has changed due to marriage or other reason – What obligations does he or she have, if any?

A Licensee is required to notify the Illinois State Police within thirty (30) days of any change of name. The Licensee must submit a notarized statement indicating that the Licensee has changed his or her name, including the prior and current name and the date the applicant changed his or her name, and pay the requisite $75 fee (as of 2014) [430 ILCS 66/55(a) and 430 ILCS 66/60(d)]. A violation of the change of name notice requirement by a Licensee is a petty offense with a fine of $150 [430 ILCS 66/55(c)].

7-104. If a Licensee believes he or she may have lost, stolen, or destroyed his or her License. What does the Licensee need to do?

A Licensee must notify the Illinois State Police within ten (10) days of discovering that his or her License has been lost, destroyed, or stolen. A lost, destroyed, or stolen License is deemed invalid. To request a replacement License, the Licensee must submit: (1) a signed and notarized statement that the Licensee no longer possesses the License, and that the License was lost, destroyed, or stolen; (2) if applicable, a copy of a police report stating that the License was stolen; and (3) payment of the requisite $75 fee (as of 2014) [430 ILCS 66/55(b) and 430 ILCS 66/60(d)]. A violation of the lost, stolen or destroyed License notice requirement by a Licensee is a petty offense with a fine of $150 [430 ILCS 66/55(c)].

7-105. Are valid License holders exempt from background checks to purchase or sell a firearm?

A License to carry a concealed firearm issued by the State of Illinois does not exempt the Licensee from the requirements of a background check, including a check of the National Instant Criminal Background Check System, upon purchase or transfer of a firearm [430 ILCS 66/85].

TRAFFIC & INVESTIGATORY STOPS BY POLICE

8-101. Is a Licensee under any obligation to notify a law enforcement officer that he or she has a concealed firearm in his or her possession? Are there any other obligations?

Yes. If an officer of a law enforcement agency initiates an investigative stop (e.g., traffic stop), of a Licensee or a non-resident carrying a concealed firearm under subsection (e) of Section 40 of the Act, upon the request of the officer the Licensee or non-resident must disclose to the officer that he or she is in possession of a concealed firearm under the Act. The Licensee must also present the License upon the request of the officer if he or she is a Licensee or present upon the request of the officer evidence under paragraph (2) of subsection (e) of Section 40 of the Act that he or she is a non-resident qualified to carry under that subsection, and identify the location of the concealed firearm.

8-102. If Licensee is merely a passenger during a traffic stop, is the Licensee required to notify the police officer that he or she has a concealed firearm on his/her person and/or is the Licensee required to comply with a law enforcement officer's request to produce my License?

During a traffic stop, any passenger within the vehicle who is a Licensee or a non-resident carrying under subsection (e) of Section 40 of the Act must comply with the requirements of this subsection (h) [430 ILCS 66/10(h)].

PROHIBITED AREAS OF FIREARMS

9-101. Where are firearms allowed or prohibited under the Act?

It is critically important that a License holder and property owners review and understand the prohibited places that, despite holding a valid License, are illegal to knowingly carry a firearm in Illinois and the rights afforded under the Act. Violating this very important part of the Act may result in criminal charges or convictions against a violator. The Act expressly lists a long list of areas and places that License holders need to familiarize themselves. In some instances or unless otherwise specifically prohibited under the Act, a Licensee may still have the right to carry a concealed firearm on or about his or her person within a vehicle into a prohibited parking lot area, subject to certain specific requirements and limitations [430 ILCS 66/55(b)]. In any event, **property owners of any of the "prohibited areas" are required to post signs stating that the carrying of firearms is prohibited** (unless the building or premises is a private residence) [430 ILCS 66/65(d)]. The signs must be clearly and conspicuously posted at the entrance of a building, premises, or real property [430 ILCS 66/65(d)]. To view an example of a statutory-compliant sign under the Act, readers can visit the Illinois State Police Conceal Carry License webpage by visiting: https://ccl4illinois.com/ccw/Public/Signage.aspx (visited 01/20/2014).

Under the Act, a Licensee is strictly prohibited from knowingly carrying a firearm on or into and of the listed "prohibited areas":

(1) Any building, real property, and parking area under the control of a public or private elementary or secondary school;

(2) Any building, real property, and parking area under the control of a pre-school or child care facility, including any room or portion of a building under the control of a pre-school or child care facility. Nothing will prevent the operator of a child care facility in a family home from owning or possessing a firearm in the home or License under this Act if no child under child care at the home is present in the home or the firearm in the home is stored in a locked container when a child under child care at the home is present in the home;

(3) Any building, parking area, or portion of a building under the control of an officer of the executive or legislative branch of government, provided that nothing will prohibit a Licensee from carrying a concealed firearm onto the real property, bikeway, or trail in a park regulated by the Department of Natural Resources or any other designated public hunting area or building where firearm possession is permitted as established by the Department of Natural Resources under Section 1.8 of the Wildlife Code;

(4) Any building designated for matters before a circuit court, appellate court, or the Illinois Supreme Court, or any building or portion of a building under the control of the Illinois Supreme Court;

(5) Any building or portion of a building under the control of a unit of local government;

(6) Any building, real property, and parking area under the control of an adult or juvenile detention or correctional institution, prison, or jail;

(7) Any building, real property, and parking area under the control of a public or private hospital or hospital affiliate, mental health facility, or nursing home;

(8) Any bus, train, or form of transportation paid for in whole or in part with public funds, and any building, real property, and parking area under the control of a public transportation facility paid for in whole or in part with public funds;

(9) Any building, real property, and parking area under the control of an establishment that serves alcohol on its premises, if more than 50% of the establishment's gross receipts within the prior 3 months is from the sale of alcohol. The owner of an establishment who knowingly fails to prohibit concealed firearms on its premises as provided in this paragraph or who knowingly makes a false statement or record to avoid the prohibition on concealed firearms under this paragraph is subject to the penalty under subsection (c-5) of Section 10-1 of the Liquor Control Act of 1934;

(10) Any public gathering or special event conducted on property open to the public that requires the issuance of a permit from the unit of local government, provided this prohibition will not apply to a Licensee who must walk through a public gathering in order to access his or her residence, place of business, or vehicle;

(11) Any building or real property that has been issued a Special Event Retailer's license as defined in Section 1-3.17.1 of the Liquor Control Act during the time designated for the sale of alcohol by the Special Event Retailer's license, or a Special use permit license as defined in subsection (q) of Section 5-1 of the Liquor Control Act during the time designated for the sale of alcohol by the Special use permit license;

(12) Any public playground;

(13) Any public park, athletic area, or athletic facility under the control of a municipality or park district. Nothing will prohibit a valid Licensee from carrying a concealed firearm while on a trail or bikeway if only a portion of the trail or bikeway includes a public park;

(14) Any real property under the control of the Cook County Forest Preserve District;

(15) Any building, classroom, laboratory, medical clinic, hospital, artistic venue, athletic venue, entertainment venue, officially recognized university-related organization property, whether owned or leased, and any real property, including parking areas, sidewalks, and common areas under the control of a public or private community college, college, or university;

(16) Any building, real property, or parking area under the control of a gaming facility licensed under the Riverboat Gambling Act or the Illinois Horse Racing Act of 1975, including an inter-track wagering location licensee;

(17) Any stadium, arena, or the real property or parking area under the control of a stadium, arena, or any collegiate or professional sporting event;

(18) Any building, real property, or parking area under the control of a public library;

(19) Any building, real property, or parking area under the control of an airport;

(20) Any building, real property, or parking area under the control of an amusement park;

(21) Any building, real property, or parking area under the control of a zoo or museum;

(22) Any street, driveway, parking area, property, building, or facility, owned, leased, controlled, or used by a nuclear energy, storage, weapons, or development site or facility regulated by the federal Nuclear Regulatory Commission. A Licensee cannot under any circumstance store a firearm or ammunition in his or her vehicle or in a compartment or container within a vehicle located anywhere in or on the street, driveway, parking area, property, building, or facility described in this paragraph. Note: This is one of the prohibited areas whereby the Act specifically prohibits Licensees from carrying a concealed firearm on or about his or her person within a vehicle into the parking area, or in the immediate area surrounding his or her vehicle [430 ILCS 66/65(b)]; and/or

(23) Any area where firearms are prohibited under federal law [430 ILCS 66/65(a)(1) – (23)]. Note: This is one of the prohibited areas whereby the Act specifically prohibits Licensees from carrying a concealed firearm on or about his or her person within a vehicle into the parking area, or in the immediate area surrounding his or her vehicle [430 ILCS 66/65(b)].

9-102. Does a Licensee have a right to carry a concealed firearm within their vehicle – what if the vehicle parks in or through a prohibited area's parking lot?

It is important to understand that under the Act, there is what the author refers to as the **"Parking Lot Exception"** in many of the designated "prohibited areas" [i.e., those areas listed above in subsections (a)(1) through (21)], a property owner cannot deny a Licensee the right to carry a concealed firearm on or about his or her person *within a vehicle* (afforded under the Act) that is in a prohibited area's parking area, and may store a firearm or ammunition concealed in a case (i.e., within the vehicle's glove compartment, console, trunk, or a firearm carrying box, shipping box, or other container) so long as it is completely enclosed, in a locked vehicle or locked container and out of plain view within the vehicle in the parking area. A Licensee is also allowed to carry a concealed firearm in the immediate area surrounding his or her vehicle within a prohibited parking lot area for the limited purpose of storing or retrieving his or her firearm within the vehicle's trunk, provided the Licensee ensures the concealed firearm is *unloaded* prior to exiting the vehicle [430 ILCS 66/65(b)]. Finally, a Licensee will not be in violation of the Act if he or she is traveling along a public right-of-way that touches or crosses any of the "prohibited areas;" a public or private community college, college, or university that prohibits concealed firearms; or any private real property that prohibits concealed firearms so long as the Licensee ensures that the concealed firearm is carried on his or her person in accordance with the provisions of the Act (as explained above) or is transported in a vehicle by the Licensee in accordance with all other applicable provisions of law [430 ILCS 66/65(c)].

SCHOOLS, COLLEGES & UNIVERSITIES

10-101. What rights or obligations do educational institutions (i.e., pre-schools, primary and secondary schools, universities, colleges, etc.) have under the Act to prohibit, limit, or allow firearms, or report individuals to law enforcement?

The Act provides significant rights for, and deference to, educational institutions to prohibit firearms and implement rules with respect to firearms on its property. Knowingly carrying a firearm into any building, real property, and parking area under the control of a pre-school, child care facility, and/or a public or private elementary or secondary school is strictly prohibited under the Act [430 ILCS 66/65(a)(1) and (2)]. Furthermore, a public or private community college, college, or university from has the right to: (1) prohibit persons from carrying a firearm within a vehicle owned, leased, or controlled by the college or university; (2) develop resolutions, regulations, or policies regarding student, employee, or visitor misconduct and discipline, including suspension and expulsion; (3) develop resolutions, regulations, or policies regarding the storage or maintenance of firearms, which must include designated areas where persons can park vehicles that carry firearms; and (4) permit the carrying or use of firearms for the purpose of instruction and curriculum of officially recognized programs, including but not limited to military science and law enforcement training programs, or in any designated area used for hunting purposes or target shooting [430 ILCS 66/65(a-5)(1) - (4)]. The Act prohibits against knowingly carrying a firearm into any building, classroom, laboratory, officially recognized university-related organization property, whether owned or leased, and any real property, including parking areas, sidewalks, and common areas under the control of a public or private community college, college, or university [430 ILCS 66/65(a)(15)]. Keep in mind that the foregoing rights and restrictions may be subject to the Parking Lot Exception.

Also, the portion of the Act referred to as the "*School Administrator Reporting of Mental Health Clear and Present Danger Determinations Law*" [430 ILCS 66/100, *et seq.*] makes it the legal duty and obligation of the principal of a public elementary or secondary school (or his or her designee), and the chief administrative officer of a private elementary or secondary school or a public or private community college, college, or university (or his or her designee) to report to the Illinois State Police when a student is determined to pose a "clear and present danger" to himself, herself, or to others, within twenty-four (24) hours of the determination (as provided in Section 6-103.3 of the Mental Health and Developmental Disabilities Code) [430 ILCS 66/105]. The term "*Clear and present danger*" means a person who: (1) communicates a serious threat of physical violence against a reasonably identifiable victim or poses a clear and imminent risk of serious physical injury to himself, herself, or another person as determined by a physician, clinical psychologist, or qualified examiner; or (2) demonstrates threatening physical or verbal behavior, such as violent, suicidal, or assaultive threats, actions, or other behavior, as determined by a physician, clinical psychologist, qualified examiner, school administrator, or law enforcement official [430 ILCS 65/1.1].

A principal or chief administrative officer, or the designee of a principal or chief administrative officer, making the determination and reporting under Section 105 of the Act has is granted immunity, and therefore, will not be held criminally, civilly, or professionally liable for reporting any such individual, except instances where the determination and reporting is determined to be willful or wanton misconduct [430 ILCS 66/110].

PRIVATE PROPERTY OWNER - RIGHTS & OBLIGATIONS

11-101. What rights do private property owners have to prohibit or allow firearms on their property?

The owner of private real property of any type may prohibit the carrying of concealed firearms on the property which is under his or her control. However, a property owner wishing to prohibit firearms on his or her property is required to clearly and conspicuously post a sign (unless the property is the owner's home or a private residence) at the entrance of a building, premises, or real property indicating that firearms are prohibited on the property under the Act [430 ILCS 66/65(a-10)]. However, these signs must strictly comply with the Act and the specific rules adopted by the Illinois State Police with respect to the standardized size, dimensions, and appearance to be valid. More specifically, the Illinois State Police rules require the sign to have: (1) a white background; (2) no text (except the reference to the Illinois Code 430 ILCS 66/1) or marking within the one-inch area surrounding the graphic design; (3) a depiction of a handgun in black ink with a circle around and diagonal slash across the firearm in red ink; and (4) the image be 4 inches in diameter. The sign in its entirety will measure 4 inches x 6 inches [430 ILCS 66/65(d)].

FEES & FISCAL ACCOUNTABILITY

12-101. Where do all the fees associated with License applications, renewals, etc. go?

The $150 application fee (as of 2014) paid by an Illinois resident for a new or renewal License is required to be apportioned in the following manner: $120 to the State Police Firearm Services Fund, $20 to the Mental Health Reporting Fund, and $10 to the State Crime Laboratory Fund [430 ILCS 66/60(b)].

The $300 non-resident (of Illinois) application fee (as of 2014) paid for a new License, or the $300 renewal License fee (both as of 2014) is required to be apportioned in the following manner: $250 to the State Police Firearm Services Fund, $40 to the Mental Health Reporting Fund, and $10 to the State Crime Laboratory Fund [430 ILCS 66/60(c)].

The $75 fee (as of 2014) paid by a Licensee due to a change of name or address, or due to a lost, stolen, or destroyed License must be apportioned in the following manner: $60 to the State Police Firearm Services Fund, $5 to the Mental Health Reporting Fund, and $10 to the State Crime Laboratory Fund [430 ILCS 66/60(d)].

The $150 fines paid by persons convicted of a violation of the Act must be deposited into the Mental Health Reporting Fund [430 ILCS 66/70(e)].

VIOLATIONS, REVOCATIONS & SUSPENSIONS

13-101. What may cause a Licensee to have his or her License invalidated, revoked, temporarily suspended, or permanently suspended by the Illinois State Police, and what are the possible administrative or criminal consequences?

(1) A License will be revoked if, at any time, the Licensee is found to be ineligible for a License under the Act [430 ILCS 66/70(a)];

(2) A License will be revoked if, at any time, the Licensee no longer meets the eligibility requirements of the FOID Card Act [430 ILCS 66/70(a)];

(3) A License will be suspended if an order of protection (including an emergency order of protection, plenary order of protection, or interim order of protection under Article 112A of the Code of Criminal Procedure of 1963 or under the Illinois Domestic Violence Act of 1986) is issued against a Licensee for the duration of the order, or if the Illinois State Police is made aware of a similar order issued against the Licensee in any other jurisdiction. If an order of protection is issued against a Licensee, the Licensee must surrender his or her License, as

applicable, to the court at the time the order of protection is entered or to the law enforcement agency or entity serving process at the time the Licensee is served the order of protection. The court, law enforcement agency, or entity responsible for serving the order of protection must notify the Illinois State Police within seven (7) days and transmit the License to the Illinois State Police [430 ILCS 66/70(b)];

(4) A License is invalid upon expiration of the License, unless the Licensee has submitted an application to renew the License, and the applicant is otherwise eligible to possess a License under the Act [430 ILCS 66/70(c)];

(5) A Licensee is prohibited from carrying a concealed firearm while under the influence of alcohol, other drug or drugs, intoxicating compound or combination of compounds, or any combination thereof, under the standards set forth in subsection (a) of Section 11-501 of the Illinois Vehicle Code. A Licensee in violation will be guilty of a Class A misdemeanor for a first or second violation and a Class 4 felony for a third violation. The Illinois State Police may suspend a License for up to six (6) months for a second violation and will permanently revoke a License for a third violation [430 ILCS 66/70(d)];

(6) Except as otherwise provided, a Licensee in violation of the Act will be guilty of a Class B misdemeanor. A second or subsequent violation is a Class A misdemeanor. The Illinois State Police may suspend a License for up to six (6) months for a second violation and will permanently revoke a License for three (3) or more violations of Section 65 (i.e., knowingly carrying a concealed firearm in any of the prohibited areas) of the Act. Any person convicted of a violation under Section 65 must pay a $150 fine, plus any applicable court costs or fees [430 ILCS 66/70(e)];

(7) A Licensee convicted or found guilty of a violation of the Act who has a valid License and is otherwise eligible to carry a concealed firearm will only be subject to the penalties under Section 70 [Violations] of the Act, and *cannot* also be subject to the criminal penalties under Section 21-6 of the Criminal Code [Class A misdemeanor where a person possesses or stores any weapon in any building or on land supported in whole or in part with public funds or in any building on such land without prior written permission from the chief security officer for such land or building - *See,* Unauthorized Possession or Storage of Weapons], paragraph (4), (8), or (10) of subsection (a) of Section 24-1 of the Criminal Code [*See,* Unlawful Use of Deadly Weapons], or subparagraph (A-5) or (B-5) of paragraph (3) of subsection (a) of Section 24-1.6 of the Criminal Code of 2012 [crime of aggravated unlawful use of a weapon - i.e., a pistol, revolver, or handgun possessed was uncased, unloaded, and the ammunition for the weapon was immediately accessible at the time of the offense]. Except for the foregoing, nothing in this

subsection prohibits the Licensee from being subjected to penalties for violations [430 ILCS 66/70(f)];

(8) A Licensee whose License is revoked, suspended, or denied must, within forty-eight (48) hours of receiving notice of the revocation, suspension, or denial surrender his or her License to the local law enforcement where he or she resides. Local law enforcement will provide the surrendering Licensee a written receipt and transmit the License to the Illinois State Police. If the Licensee whose License has been revoked, suspended, or denied fails to surrender his or her License to local law enforcement, such law enforcement agency may then petition the Circuit Court to issue a warrant to search for and seize the License in the possession and under the custody or control of the Licensee whose License has been revoked, suspended, or denied. The observation of a License in the possession of a person whom License has been revoked, suspended, or denied constitutes a sufficient basis for the arrest of that person. Furthermore, the failure or refusal of a Licensee to surrender his or her License when revoked, suspended, or denied within forty-eight (48) hours of receiving notice is a Class A misdemeanor [430 ILCS 66/70(g)].

(9) A License will be revoked if, at any time, a Licensee is ineligible for, or no longer possesses, a valid FOID Card (unless the Licensee has already filed a renewal application with the Illinois State Police for a Firearm Owner's Identification Card and is not ineligible to obtain a renewal Firearm Owner's Identification Card for any other reason). A Licensee whose License is revoked due to ineligibility or no longer possessing a valid FOID Card must surrender his or her License within forty-eight (48) hours of receiving notice of revocation to the local law enforcement where he or she resides [430 ILCS 66/70(g)].

13-102. Does an applicant have any appeal rights in the event of a revoked or suspended License?

Yes, whenever a License is revoked or suspended, the aggrieved party may appeal to the Director of the Illinois State Police for a hearing [430 ILCS 66/87(a)].

13-103. What are the consequences of teaching firearm training courses when *not* properly certified by the Illinois State Police?

A person who is not a certified firearms instructor are prohibited from teaching applicant firearm training courses, advertise, or otherwise represent courses they teach as qualifying their students to meet the Firearms Training requirements to receive a License under the Act. Each violation is deemed a business offense subject to a fine of at least $1,000 per violation [430 ILCS 66/80(b)].

CERTIFIED FIREARMS TRAINING INSTRUCTOR QUALIFICATIONS

14-101. What are the requirements to become an Illinois State Police-approved firearms instructor under the Act?

Instructor applicants are required to electronically submit fingerprints through an Illinois licensed *Livescan* vendor in order to expedite the background check process. Electronic fingerprint submission is necessary to ensure timely approval of instructors and allow individuals who want to apply for a License access to the required Firearms Training.

Instructor applicants seeking to become a certified Illinois Concealed Carry Firearms Instructor must:

(1) be at least twenty-one (21) years of age [430 ILCS 66/80(c)(1)];

(2) be a legal resident of the United States [430 ILCS 66/80(c)(2)];

(3) possess or be eligible for a valid FOID card [430 ILCS 66/80(c)(3)];

(4) be eligible for a License in Illinois [430 ILCS 66/80(c)(3)];

(5) possess a high school diploma or General Educational Development (GED) certificate [430 ILCS 66/80(d)(1)]; and

(6) have at least one of the following valid firearms instructor certifications [430 ILCS 66/80(d)(2)]: (A) Certification from a law enforcement agency; (B) Certification from a firearm instructor course offered by a state or federal governmental agency; (C) Certification from a firearm instructor course offered by the Illinois Law Enforcement Training and Standards Board; or (D) Certification from an entity approved by the Illinois State Police that offers firearm instructor education and training in the use and safety of firearms (e.g., the National Rifle Association of America (NRA)).

14-102. What are grounds for a denial or revocation to be certified by the Illinois State Police as a certified Illinois Concealed Carry Firearms Instructor?

A person may have his or her firearms instructor certification denied or revoked if he or she does not meet the requirements to obtain a License under the Act, provides false or misleading information to the Illinois State Police, or has had a prior instructor certification revoked or denied by the Illinois State Police [430 ILCS 66/80(e)].

14-103. What are the consequences of a person teaching firearm training courses who is *not* properly certified by the Illinois State Police?

A person who is not a certified firearms instructor are prohibited from teaching applicant firearm training courses, advertise, or otherwise represent courses they teach as qualifying their students to meet the Firearms Training requirements to receive a License under the Act. Each violation is deemed a business offense subject to a fine of at least $1,000 per violation [430 ILCS 66/80(b)].

LOCAL GOVERNMENTS

15-101. Do local (Illinois) municipalities, cities, villages, townships, etc. have the right to impose stricter limitations on the right to carry or possess concealed firearms than what is required under the Act? In other words, can Home Rule powers prevail over the rights and limitations provided under the Act?

No, the regulation, licensing, possession, registration, and transportation of handguns and ammunition for handguns by Licensees are exclusive powers and functions of the State of Illinois. Therefore, any ordinance or regulation, or portion thereof, enacted on or before the effective date of the Act (i.e., July 9, 2013) that purports to impose regulations or restrictions on Licensees or handguns and ammunition for handguns in a manner inconsistent with the Act will be invalid in its application to Licensees. Section 90 of the Act serves as a clear denial and limitation of local governments to exercise Home Rule powers and functions afforded under Article VII of the Illinois Constitution [430 ILCS 66/90]. However, the Act is silent as to a local government's right to impose ordinances, rules, and/or laws regulating the local taxation of sales and purchases of firearms.

CONCEALED CARRY LICENSE AND THE FOID CARD

16-101. Is there any plan to somehow consolidate the Concealed Carry License and the FOID Card?

Yes, the Director of the Illinois State Police is required to create a "task force" to develop a plan to incorporate and consolidate the concealed carry License under the Act and the FOID Card under the FOID Card Act into a designation on the Illinois driver's license or Illinois identification card of a person with authority to possess a firearm under the FOID Card Act, or authority to possess a firearm under the FOID Card Act and authority to carry a concealed firearm under the Act. The task force is required to file the plan supported by a majority of its members with the Illinois General Assembly and the Illinois Secretary of State on or before March 1, 2014.

The plan must provide for an alternative card for: (1) a non-resident or a resident without an Illinois driver's license or Illinois identification card, who has been granted authority under the

Act to carry a concealed firearm in Illinois; and (2) a resident without an Illinois driver's license or Illinois identification card, who has been granted authority to possess a firearm under the FOID Card Act. The plan must also include statutory changes necessary to implement it.

The Act requires that the task force consist of the following members: (1) one member appointed by the Speaker of the Illinois House of Representatives; (2) one member appointed by the Illinois House of Representatives Minority Leader; (3) one member appointed by the President of the Illinois Senate; (4) one member appointed by the Illinois Senate Minority Leader; (5) one member appointed by the Illinois Secretary of State; (6) one member appointed by the Director of the Illinois State Police; (7) one member appointed by the Illinois Secretary of State representing the NRA; (8) one member appointed by the Governor of Illinois from the Illinois Department of Natural Resources; and (9) one member appointed by the Governor of Illinois representing the Chicago Police Department. The task force must elect a chairperson from its membership and members of the task force must serve without compensation [430 ILCS 66/92]. Section 92 of the Act is set to be repealed on March 2, 2014.